Nurse Coloring Book Belongs To:

____

COLOR TEST PAGE

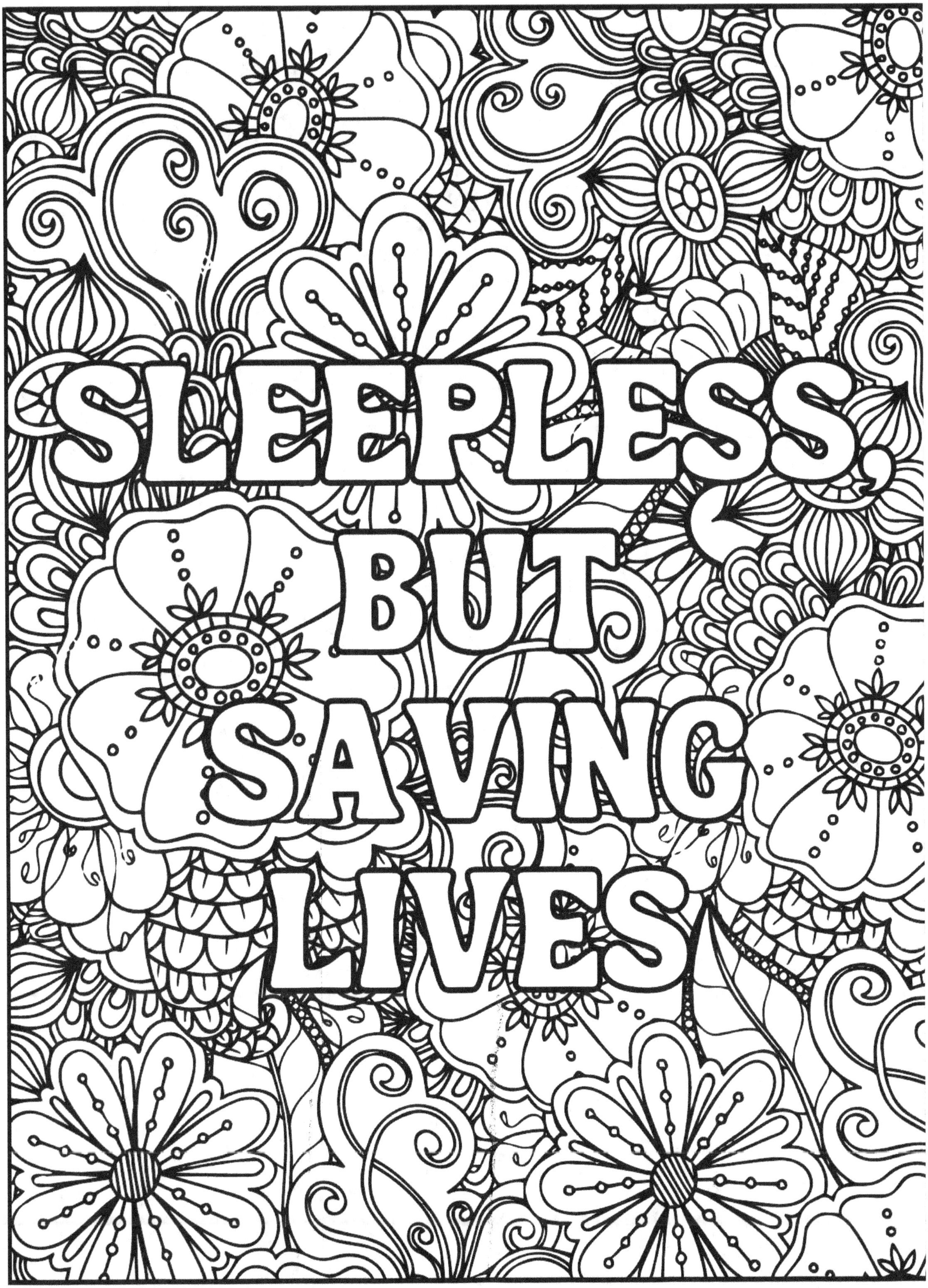
SLEEPLESS,
BUT
SAVING
LIVES

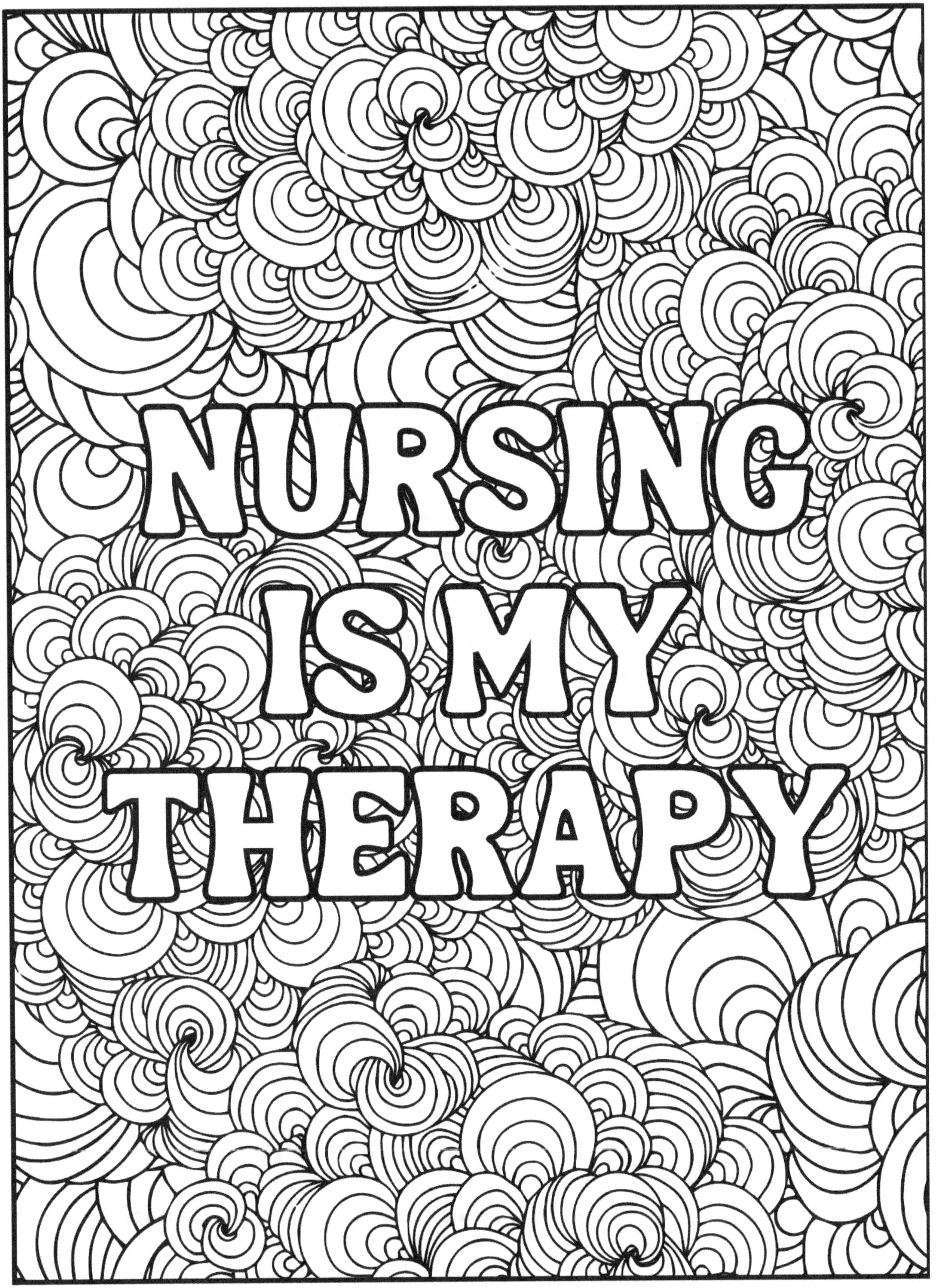
NURSING
IS MY
THERAPY

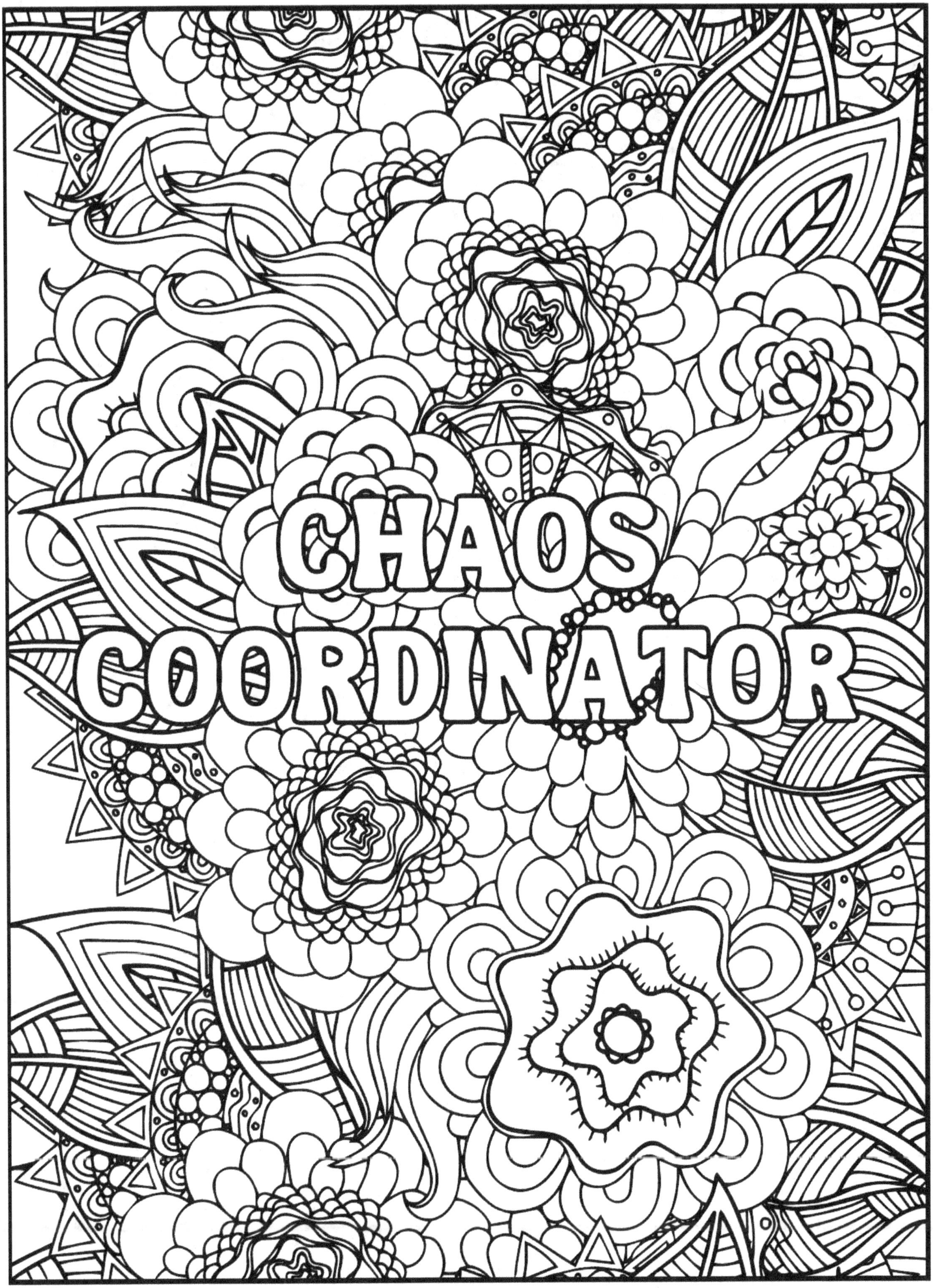
CHAOS
COORDINATOR

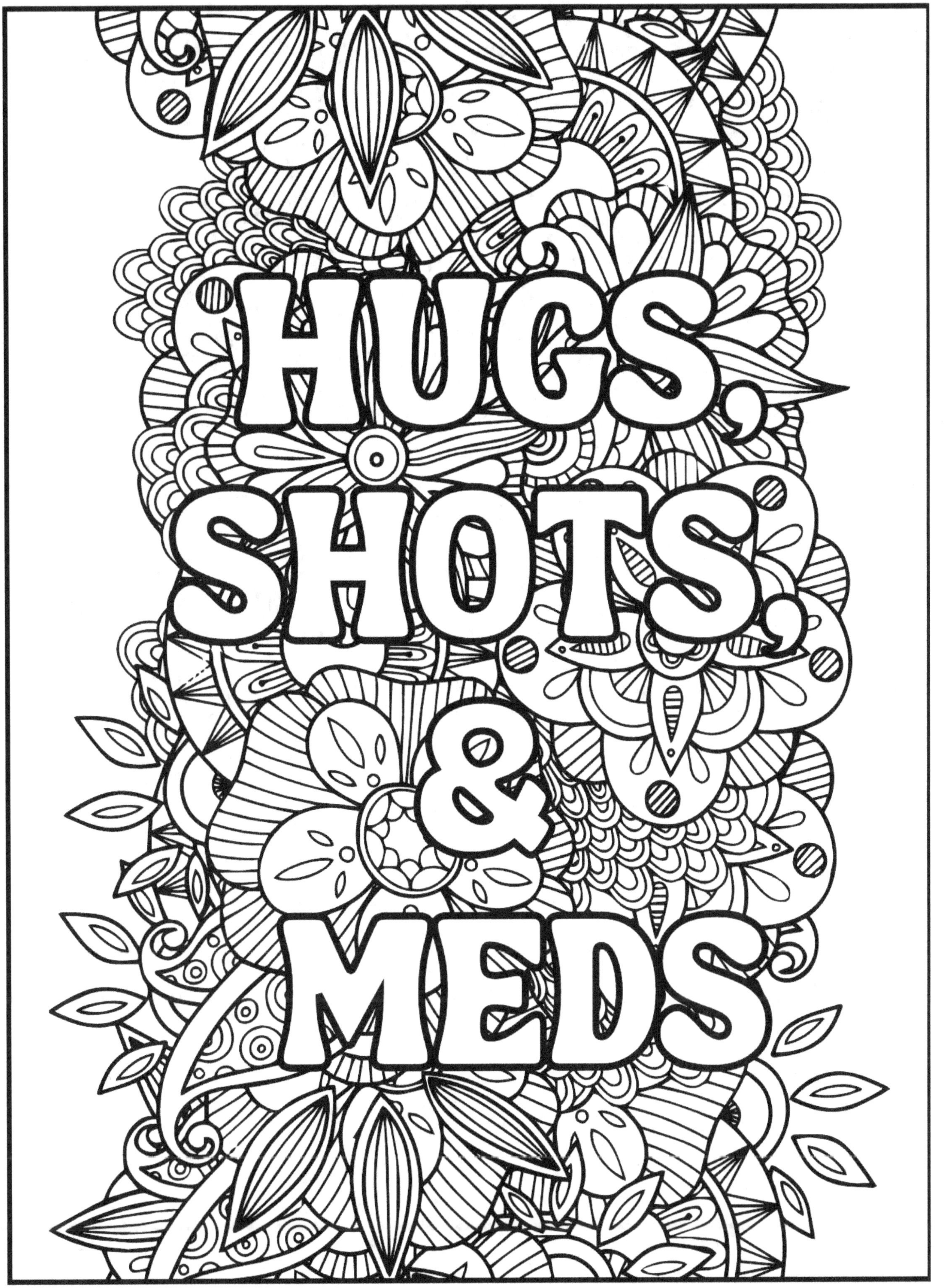
HUGS,
SHOTS,
&
MEDS

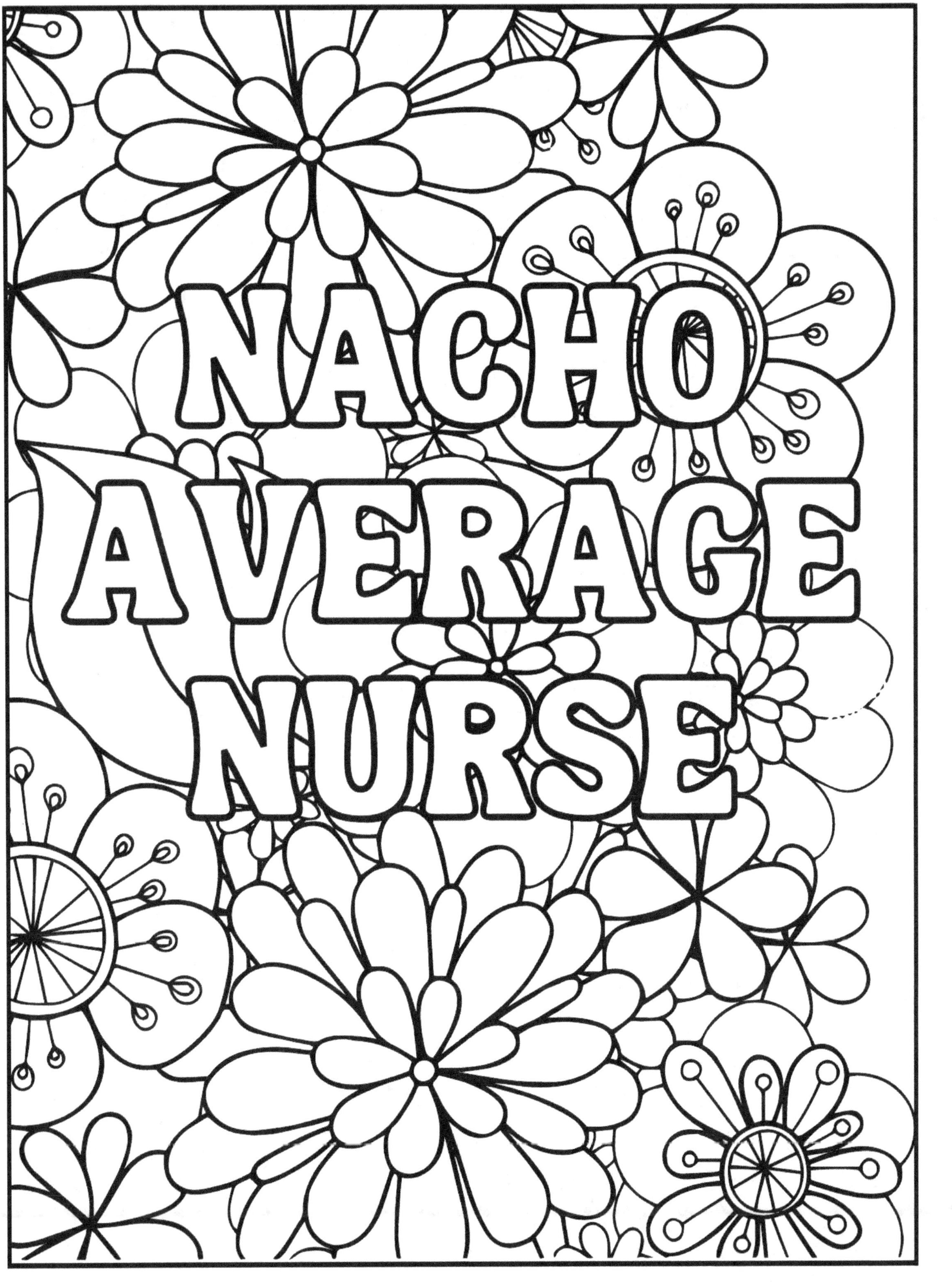
NACHO
AVERAGE
NURSE

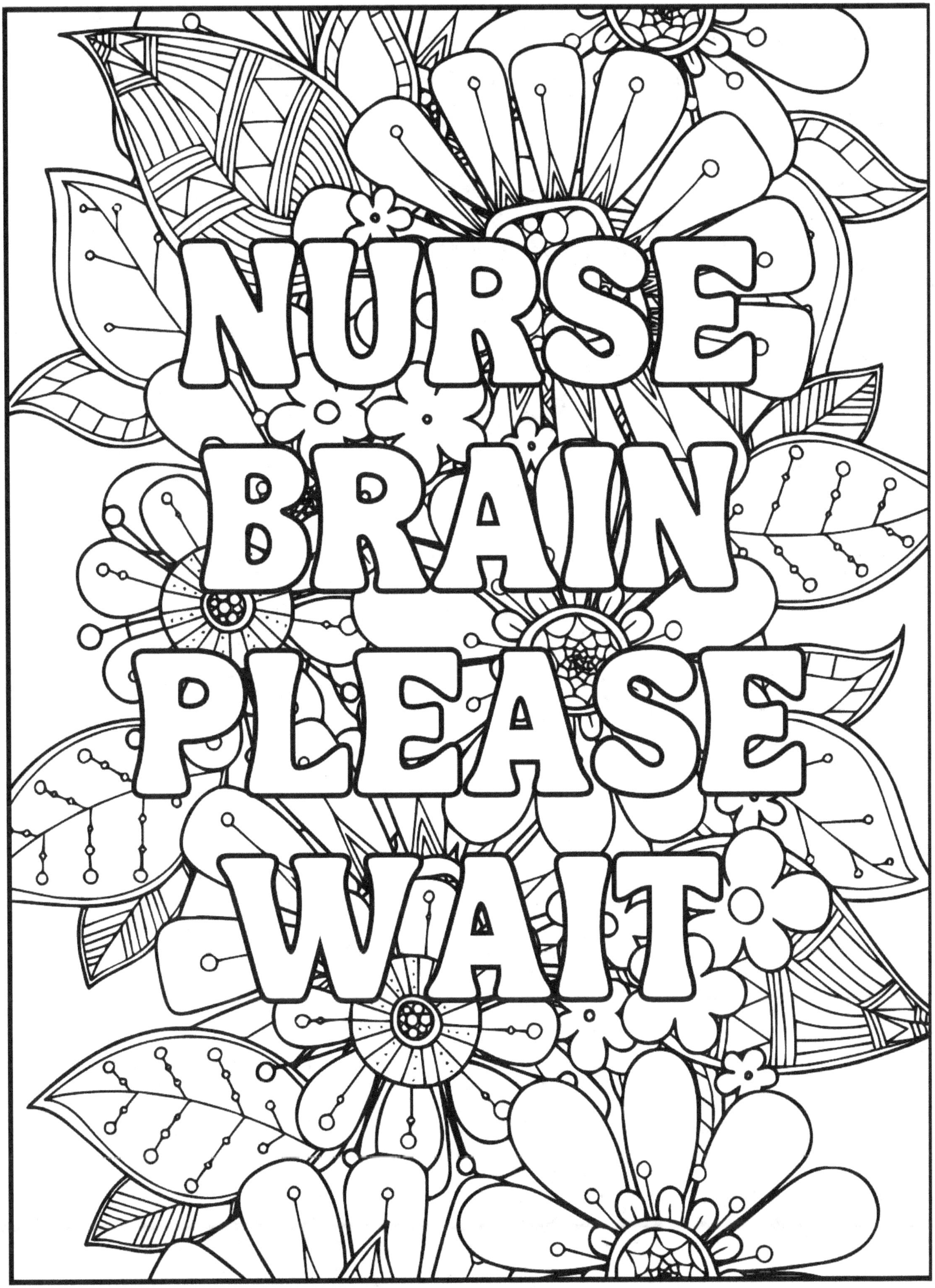
NURSE
BRAIN
PLEASE
WAIT

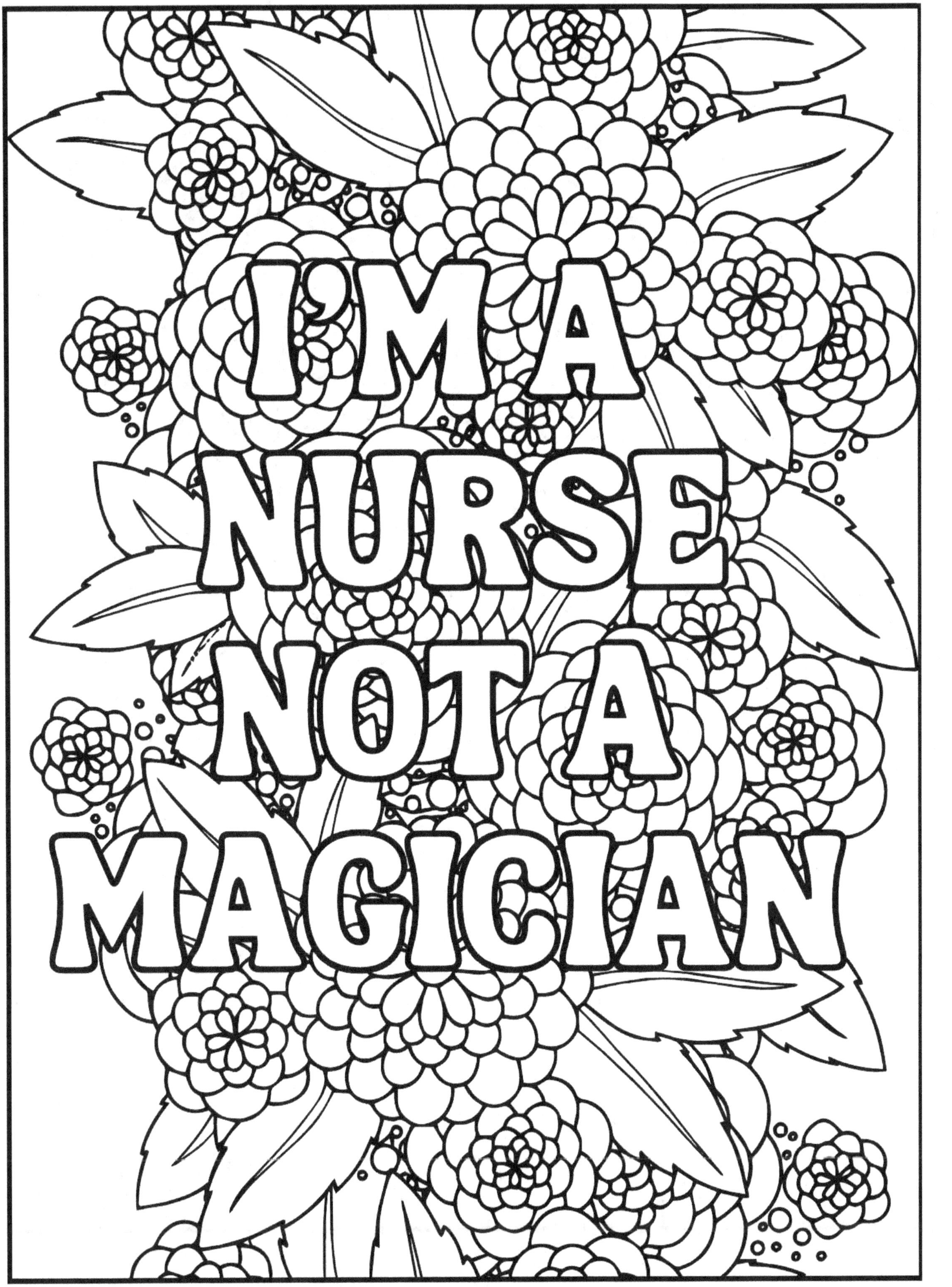
I'M A
NURSE
NOT A
MAGICIAN

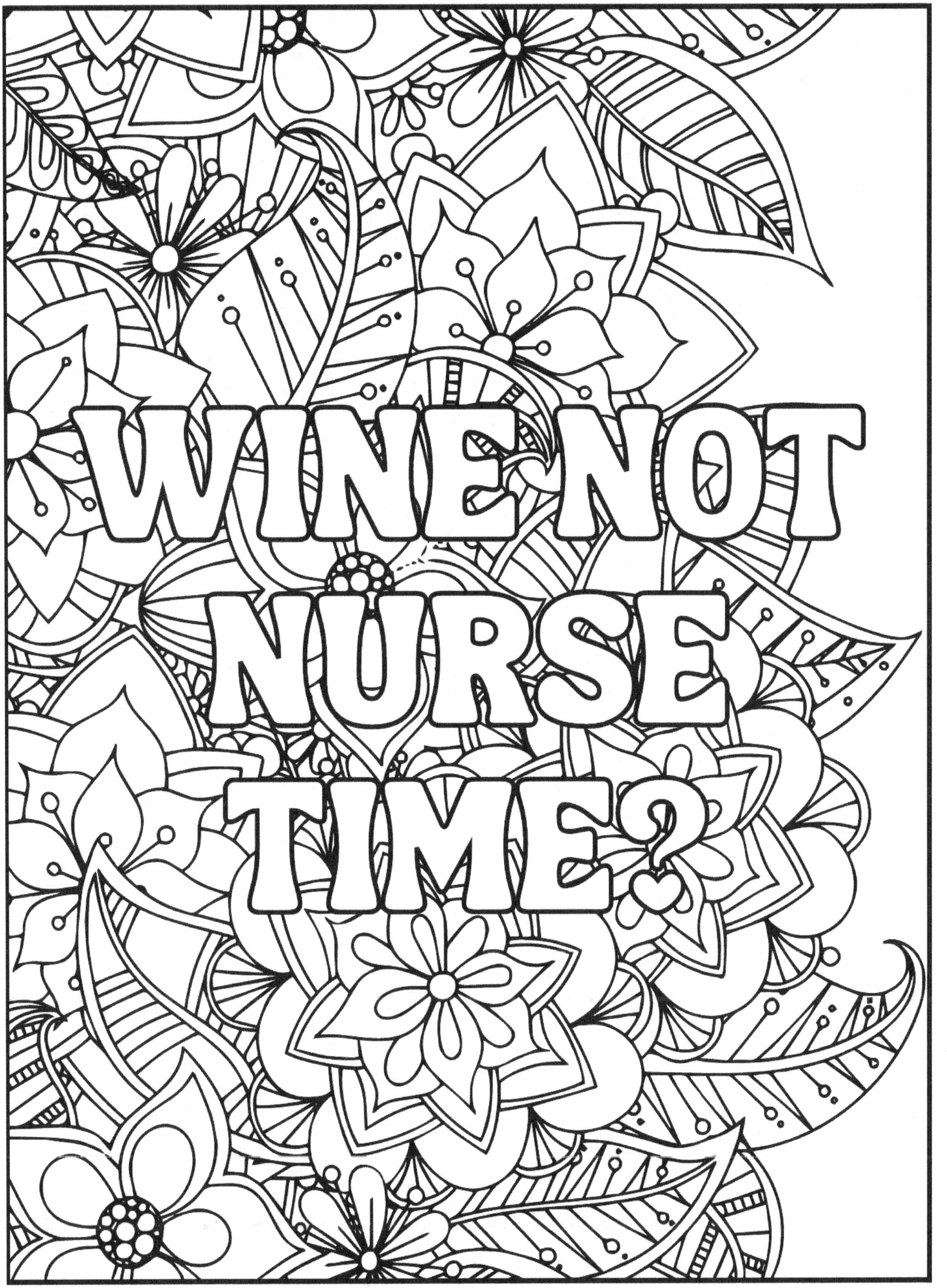
WINE NOT
NURSE
TIME?

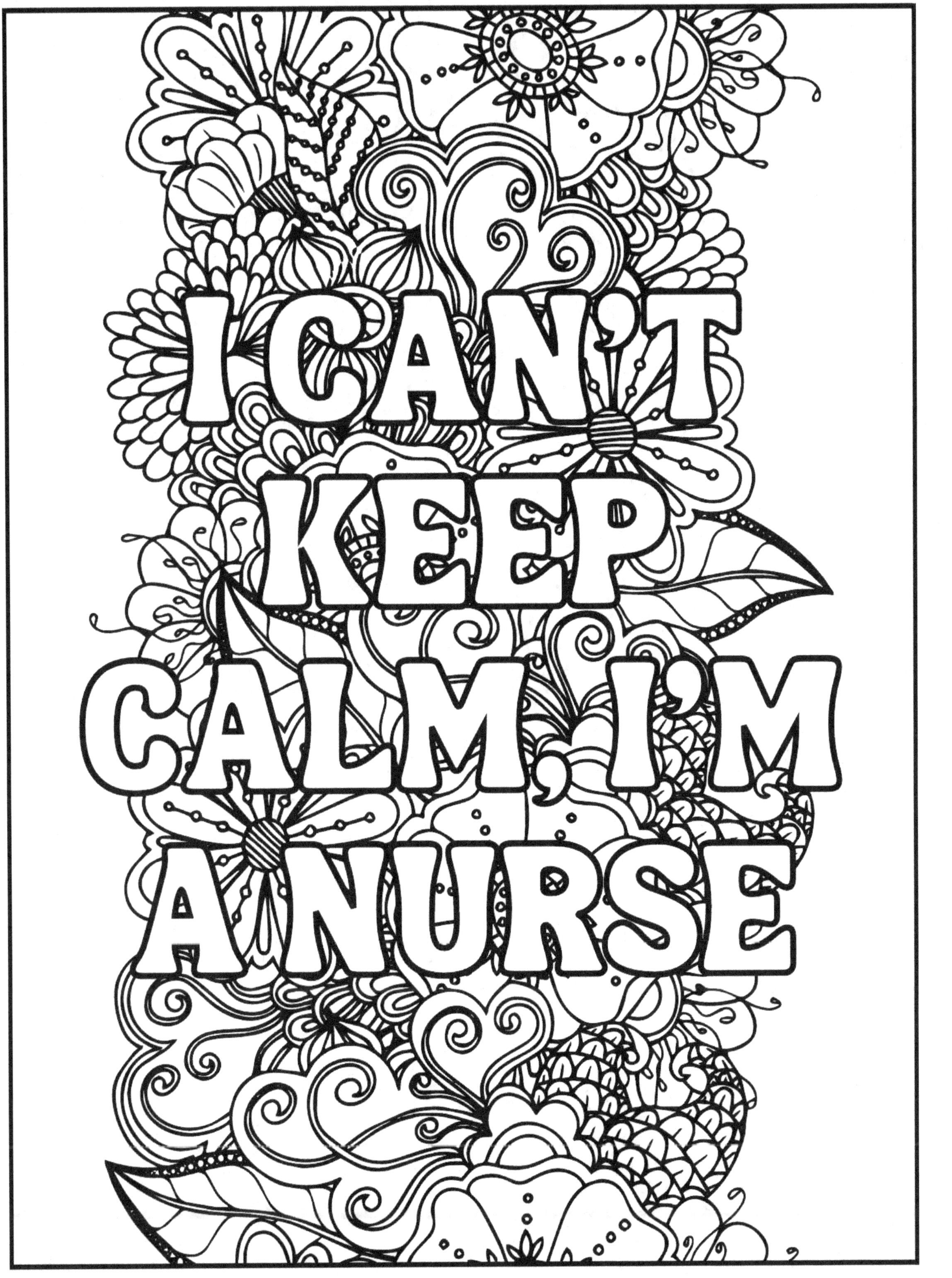
I CAN'T
KEEP
CALM, I'M
A NURSE

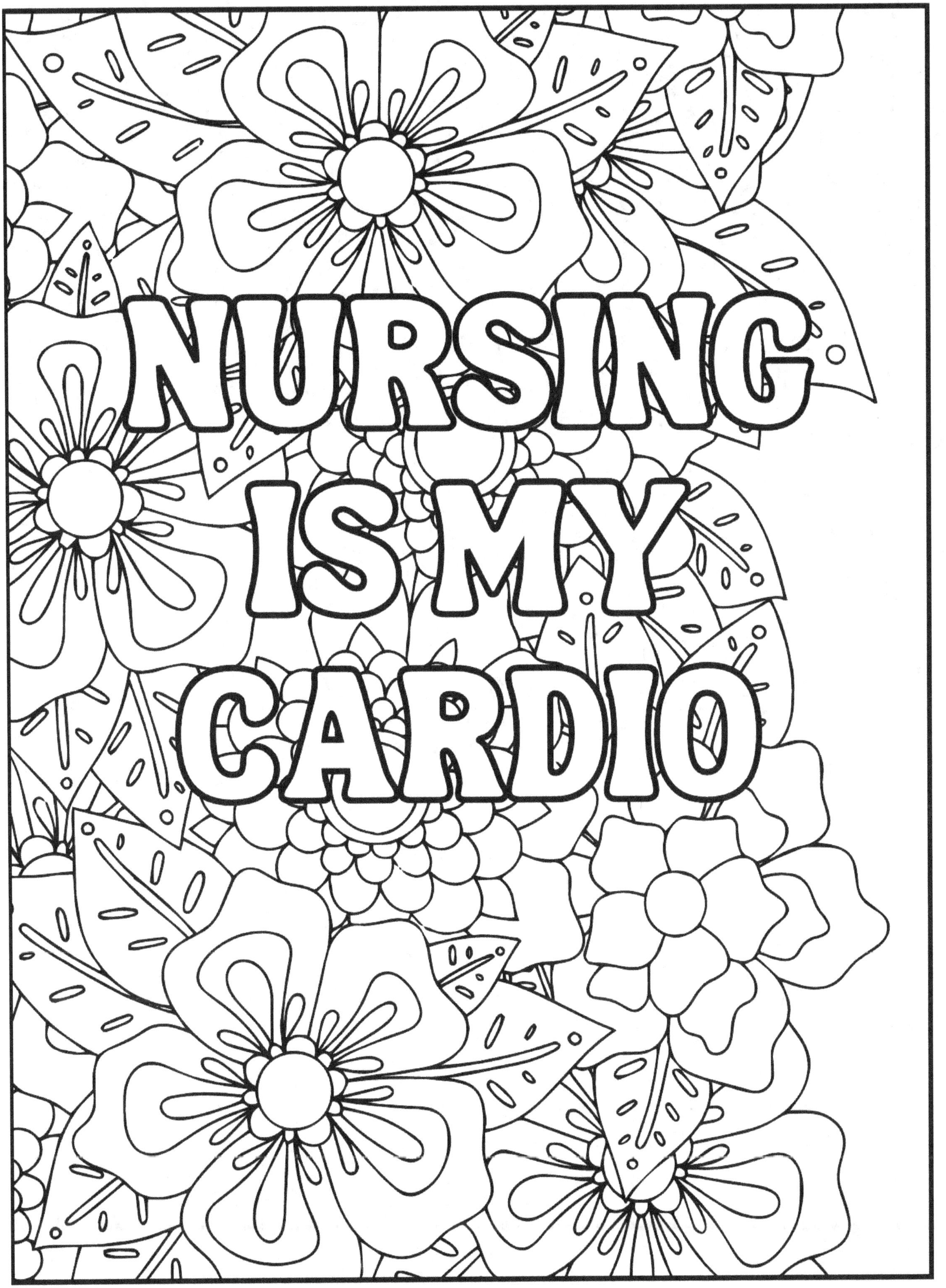
NURSING
IS MY
CARDIO

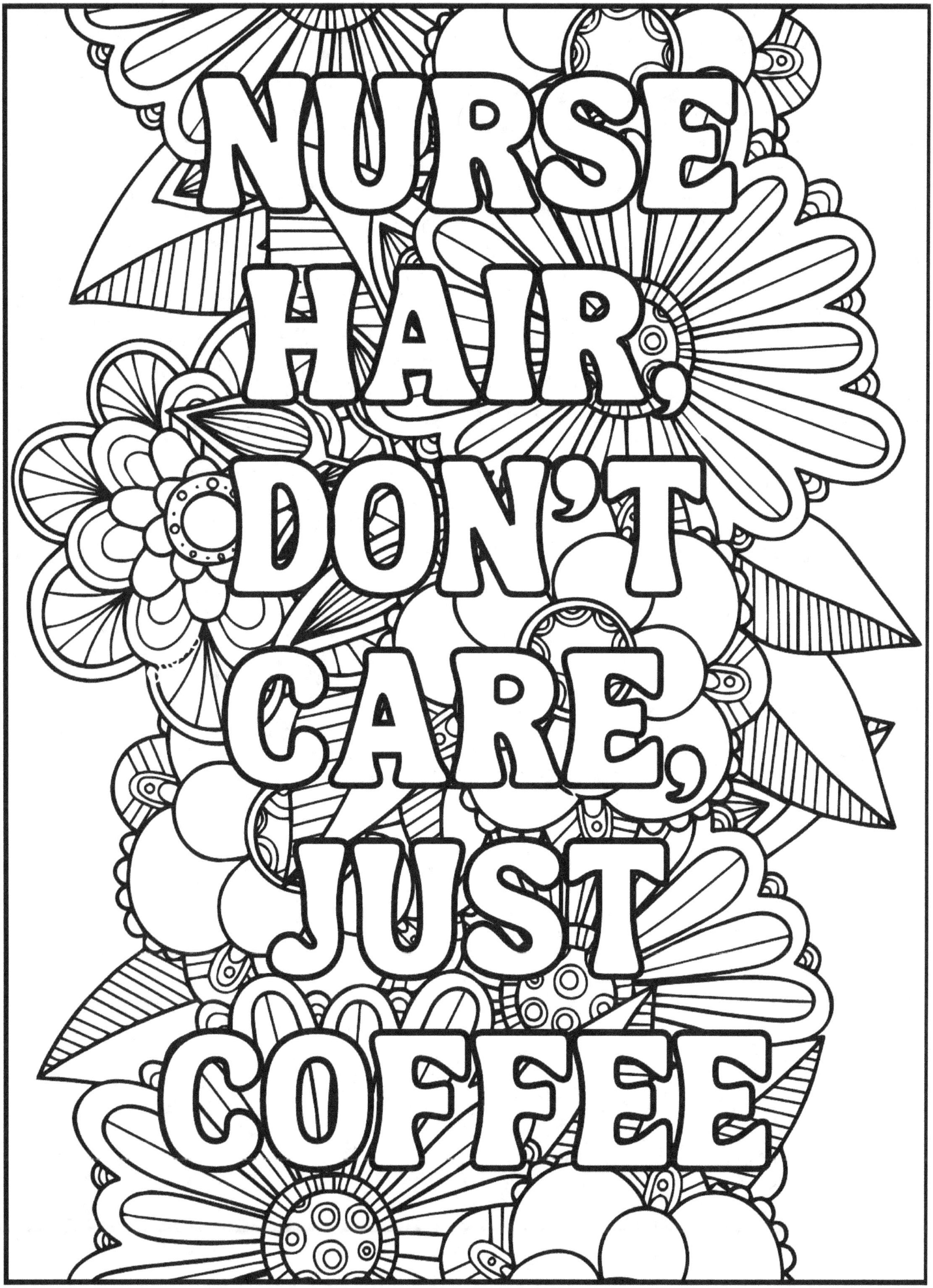
NURSE
HAIR,
DON'T
CARE,
JUST
COFFEE

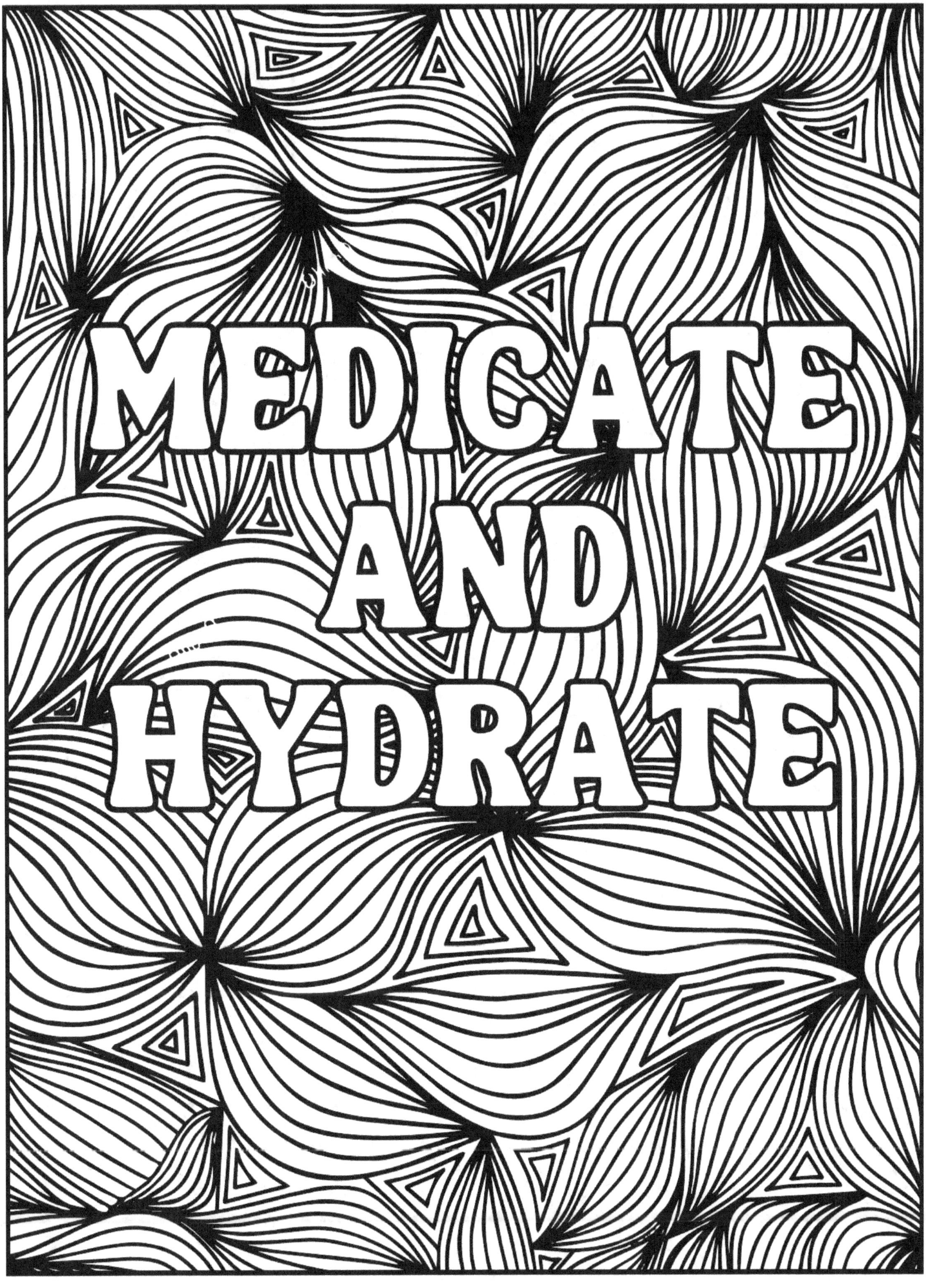
MEDICATE
AND
HYDRATE

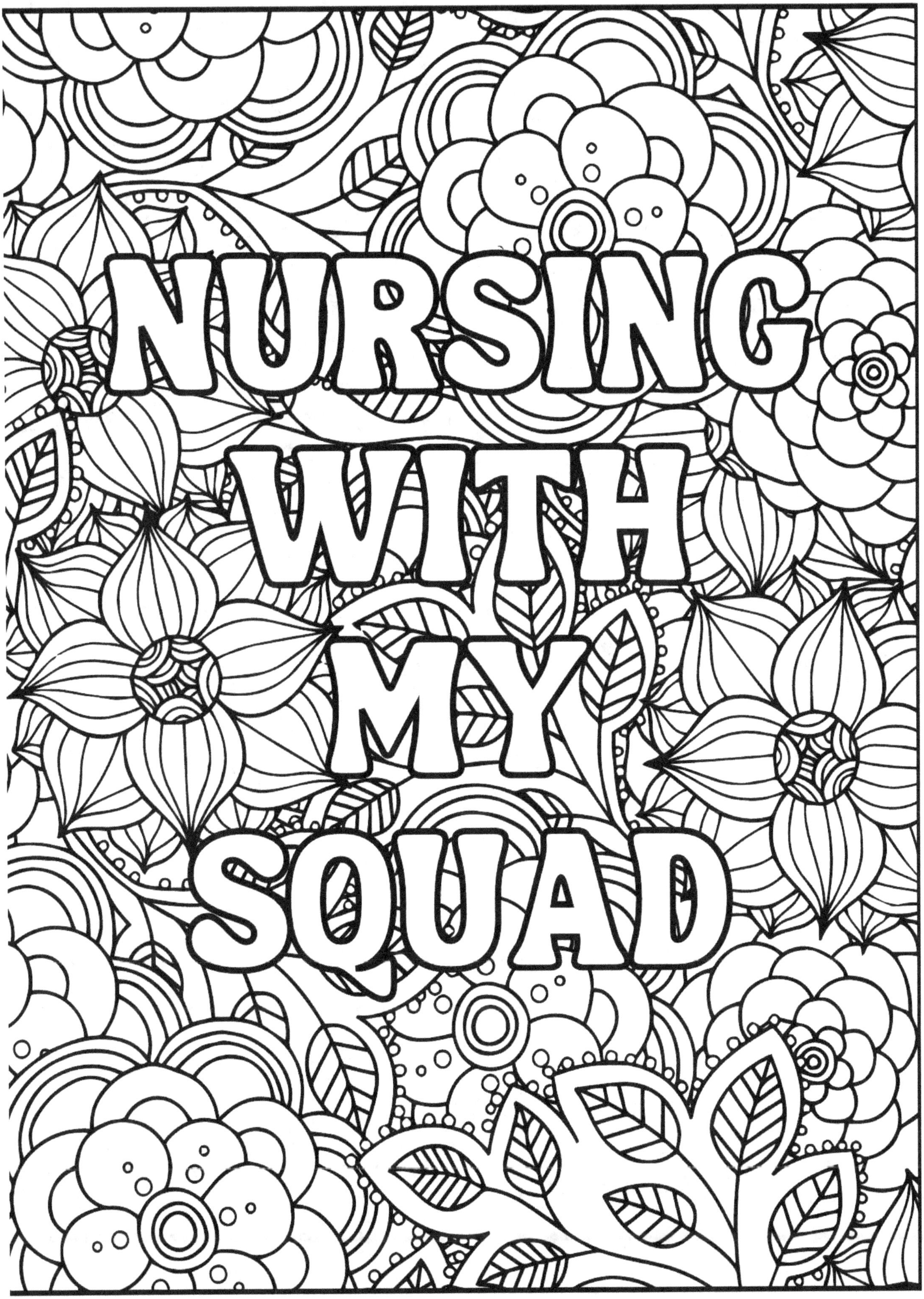
NURSING
WITH
MY
SQUAD

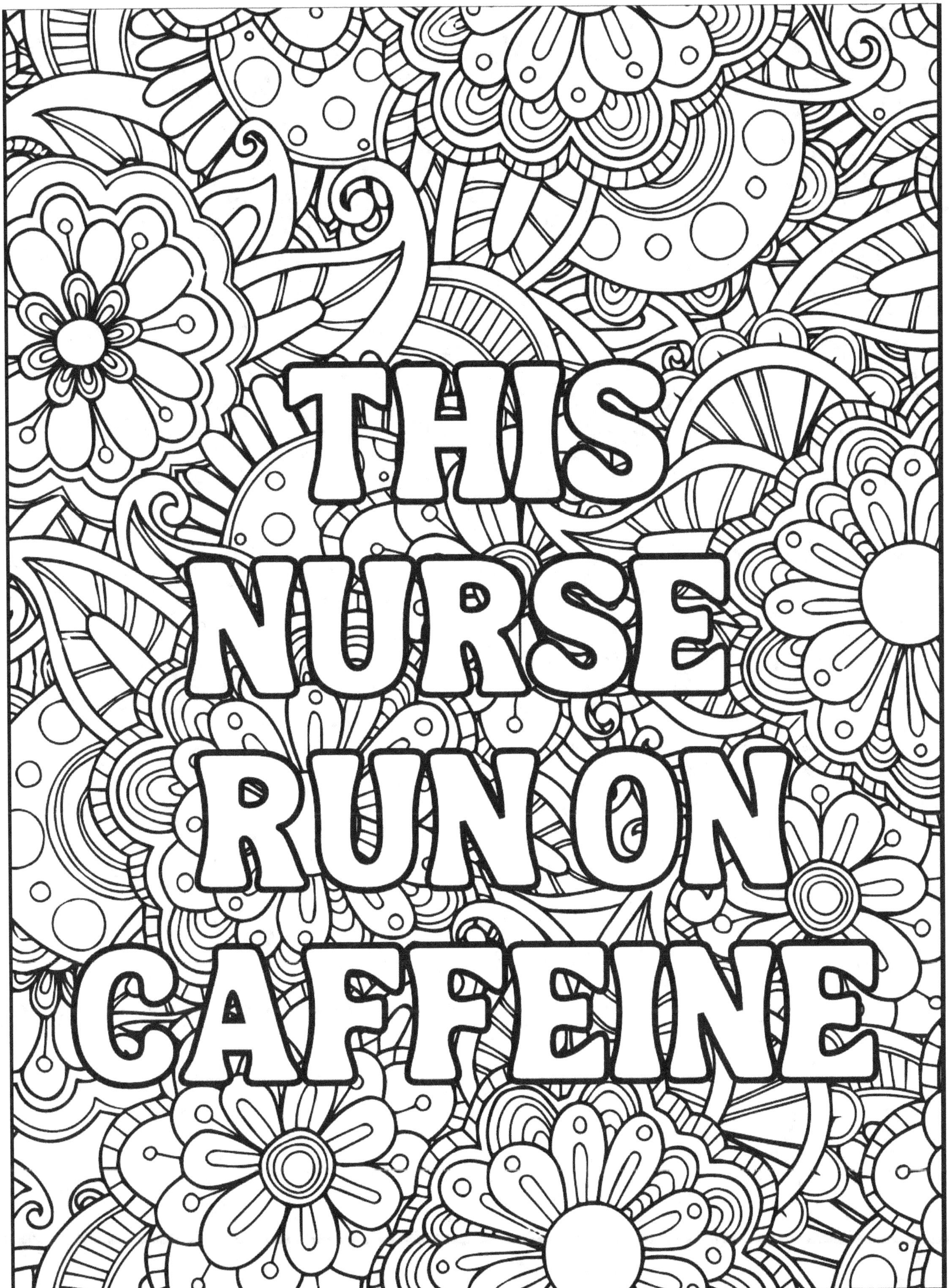
THIS
NURSE
RUN ON
CAFFEINE

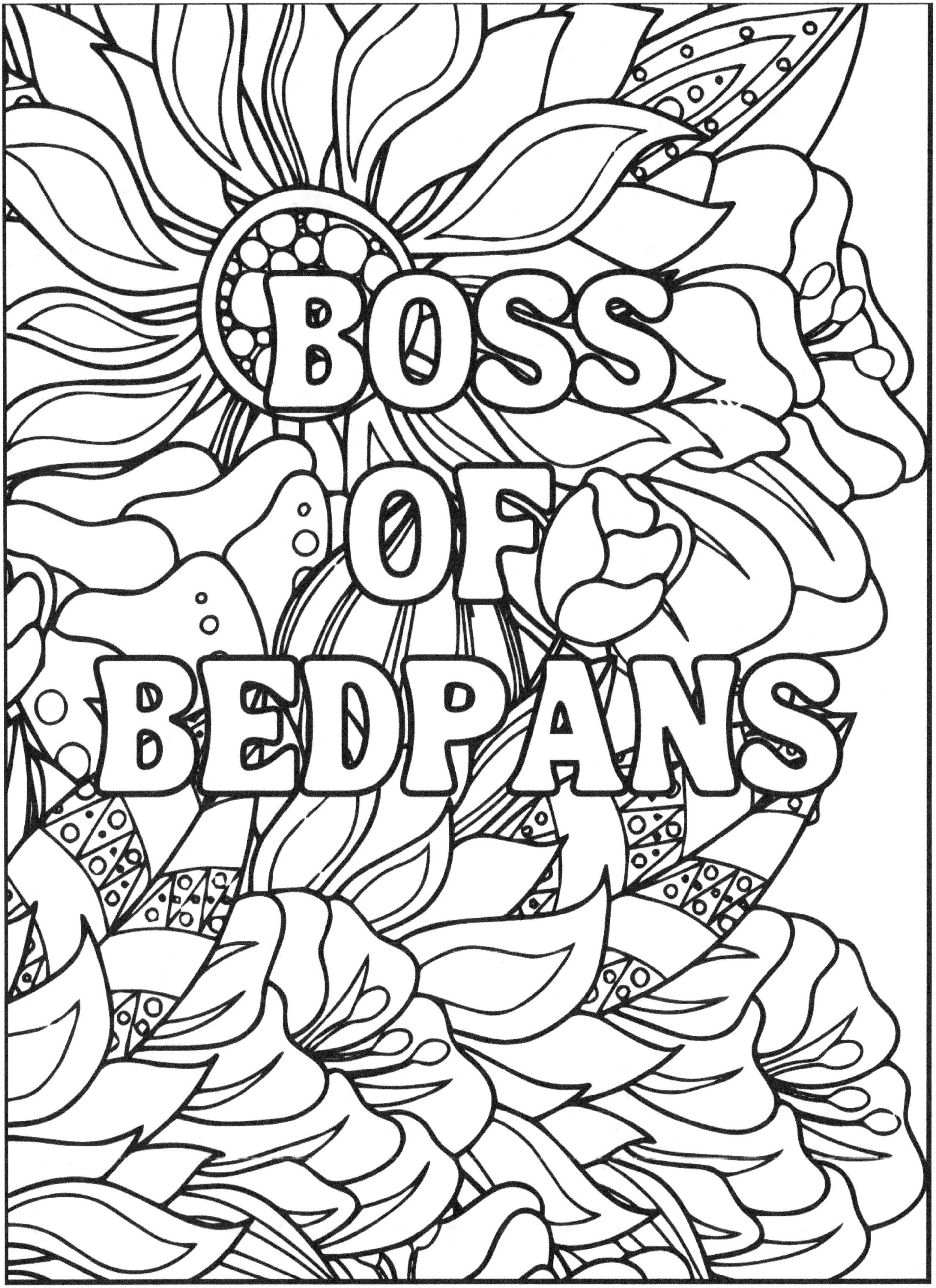
BOSS
OF
BEDPANS

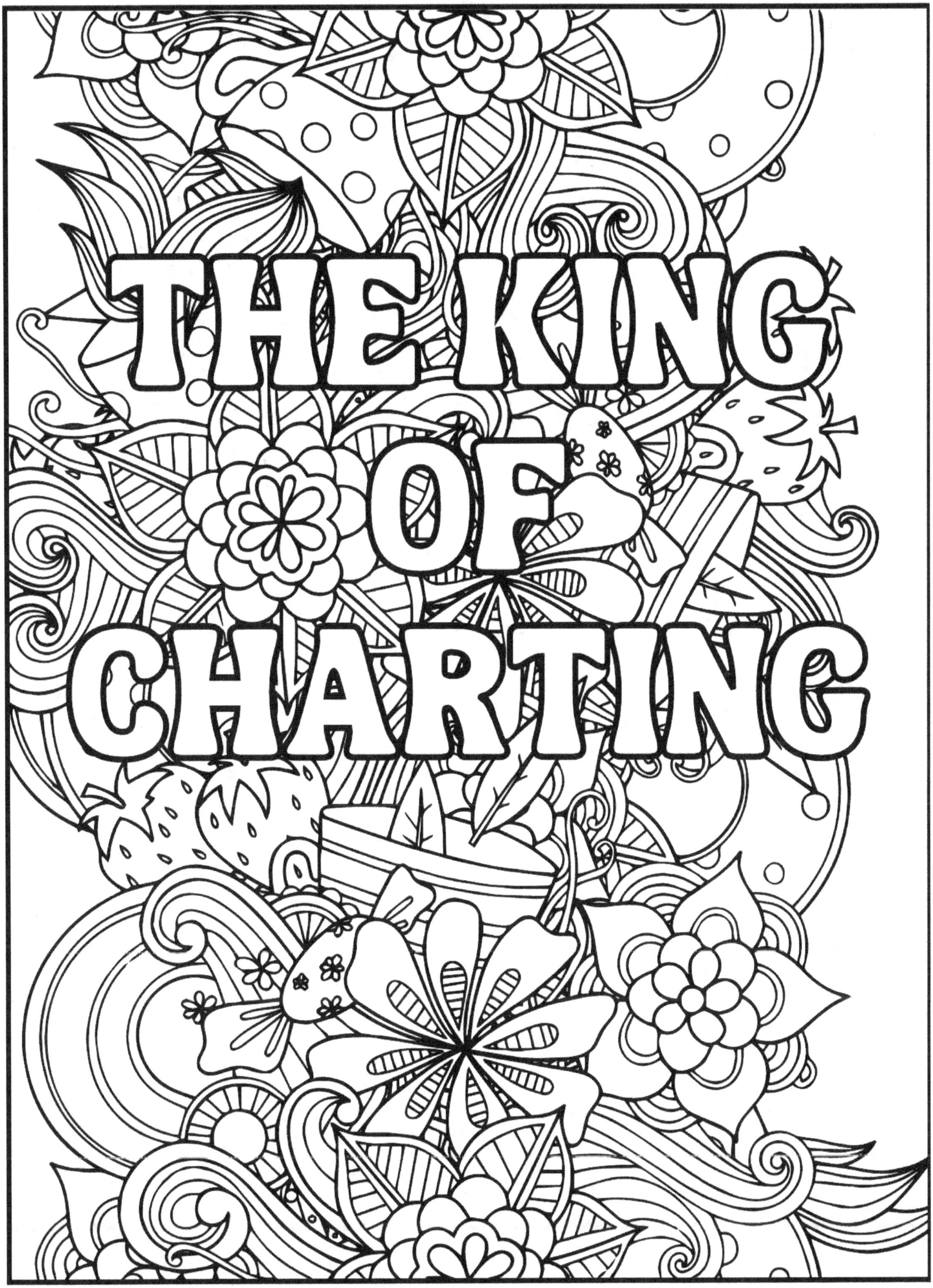
THE KING
OF
CHARTING

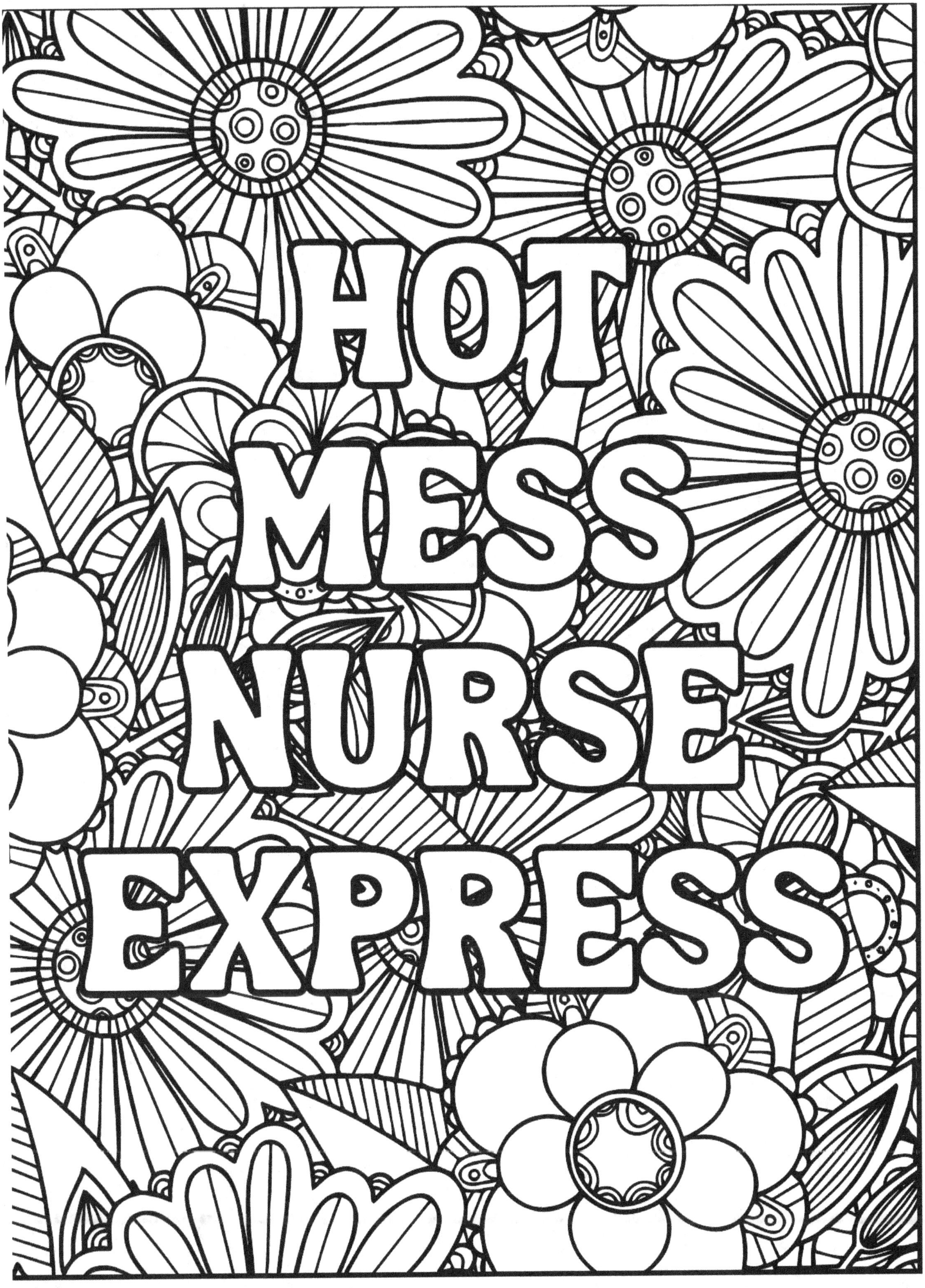
HOT
MESS
NURSE
EXPRESS

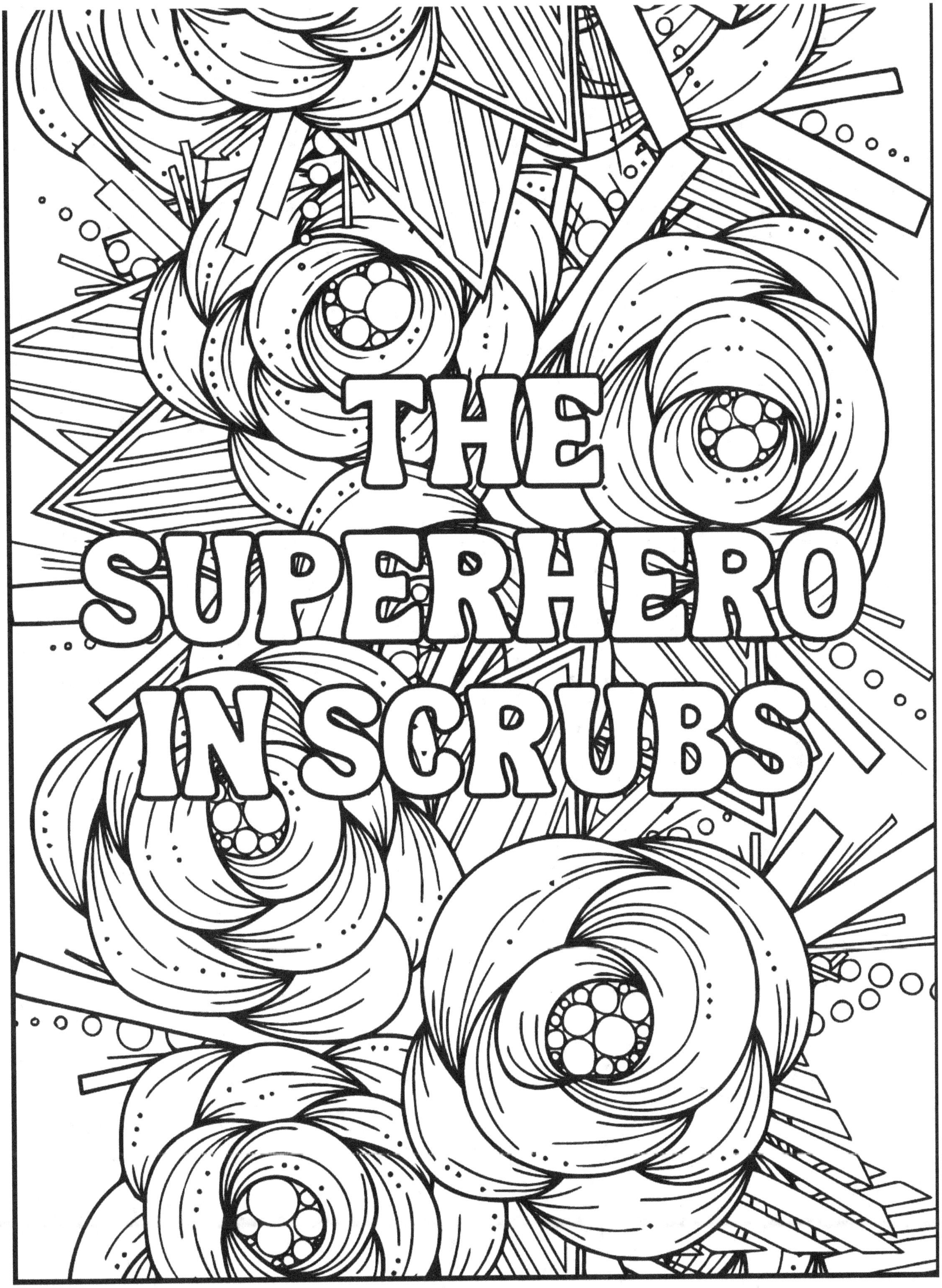
THE SUPERHERO IN SCRUBS

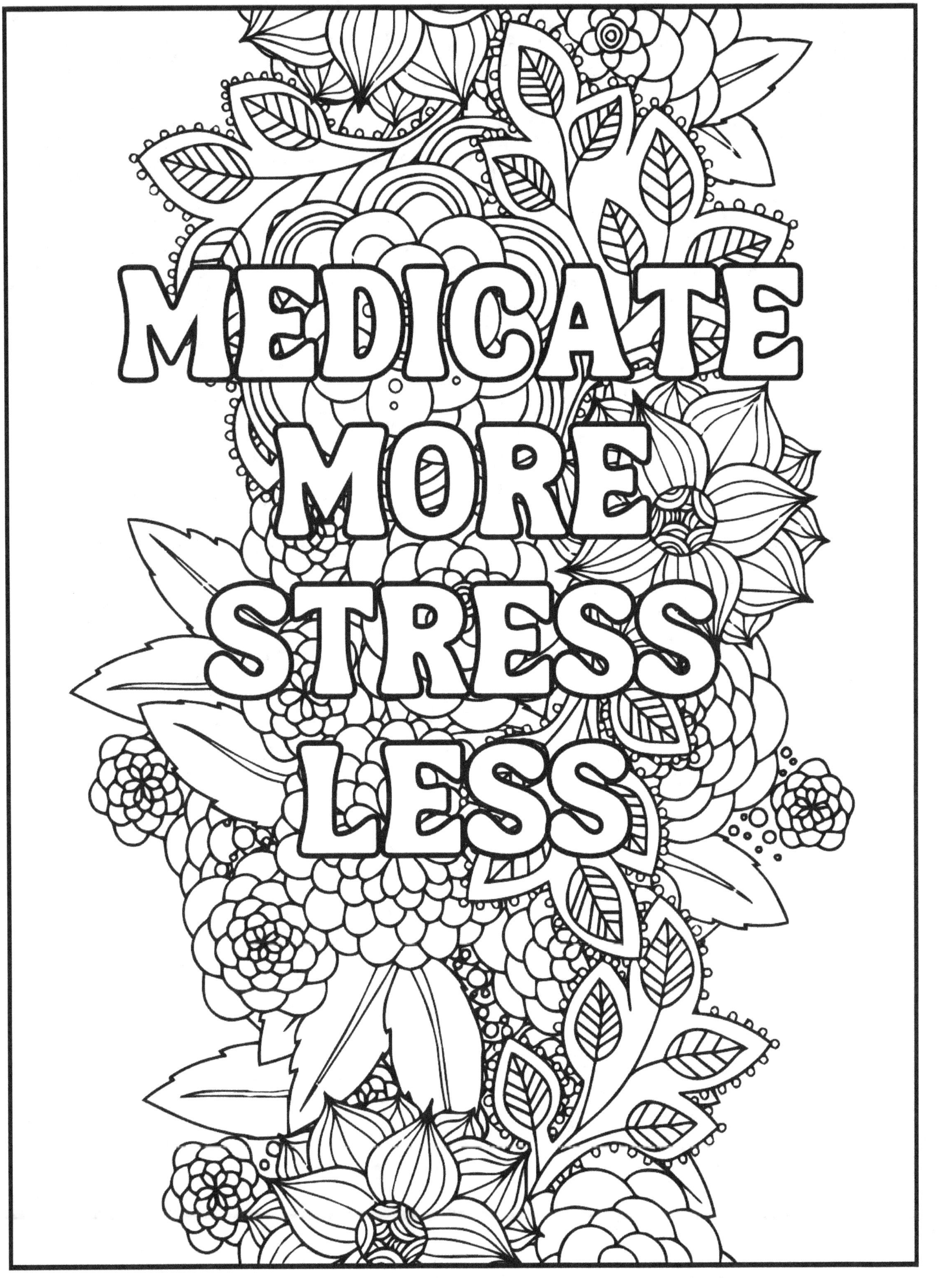
MEDICATE
MORE
STRESS
LESS

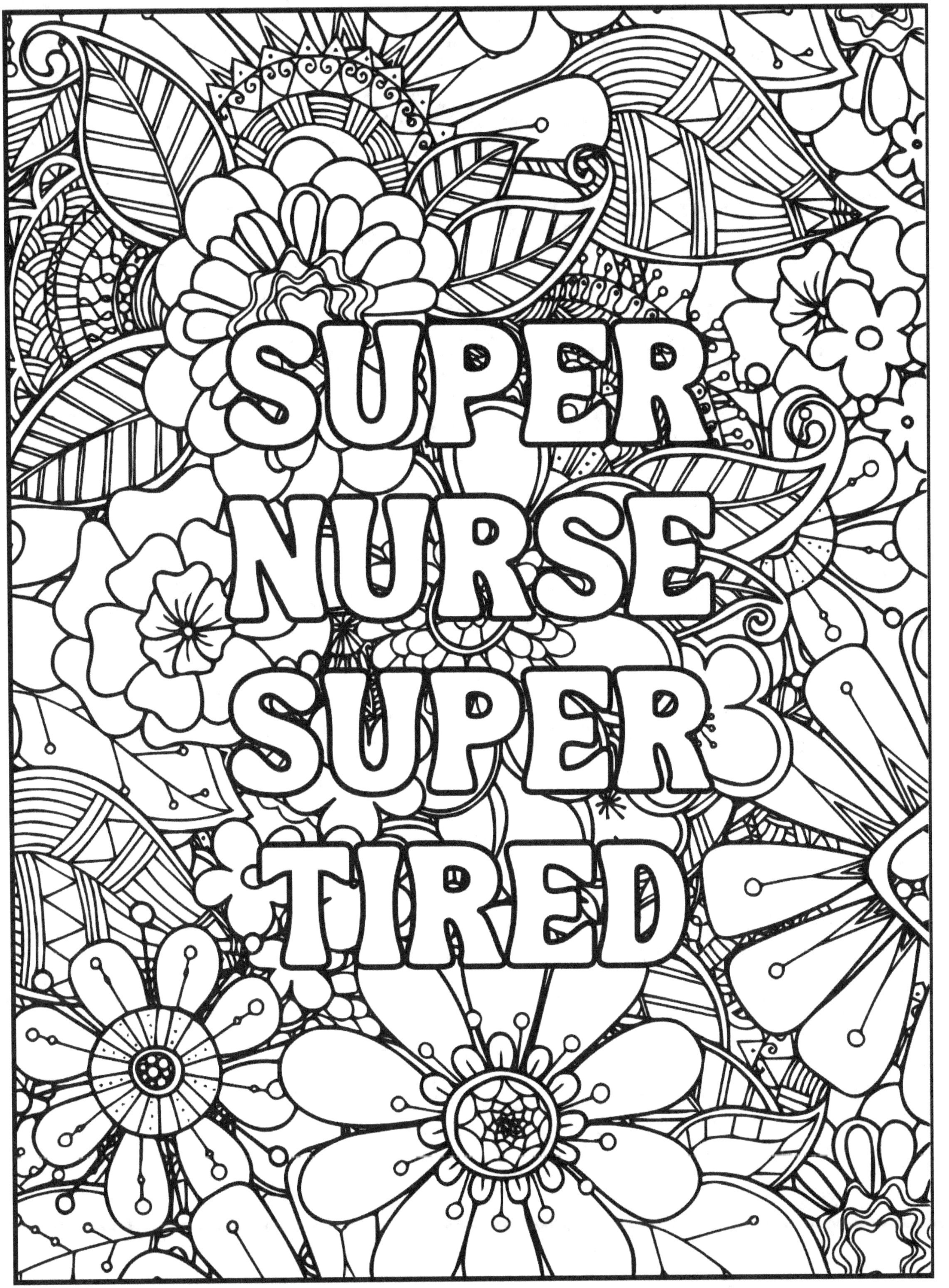
SUPER
NURSE
SUPER
TIRED

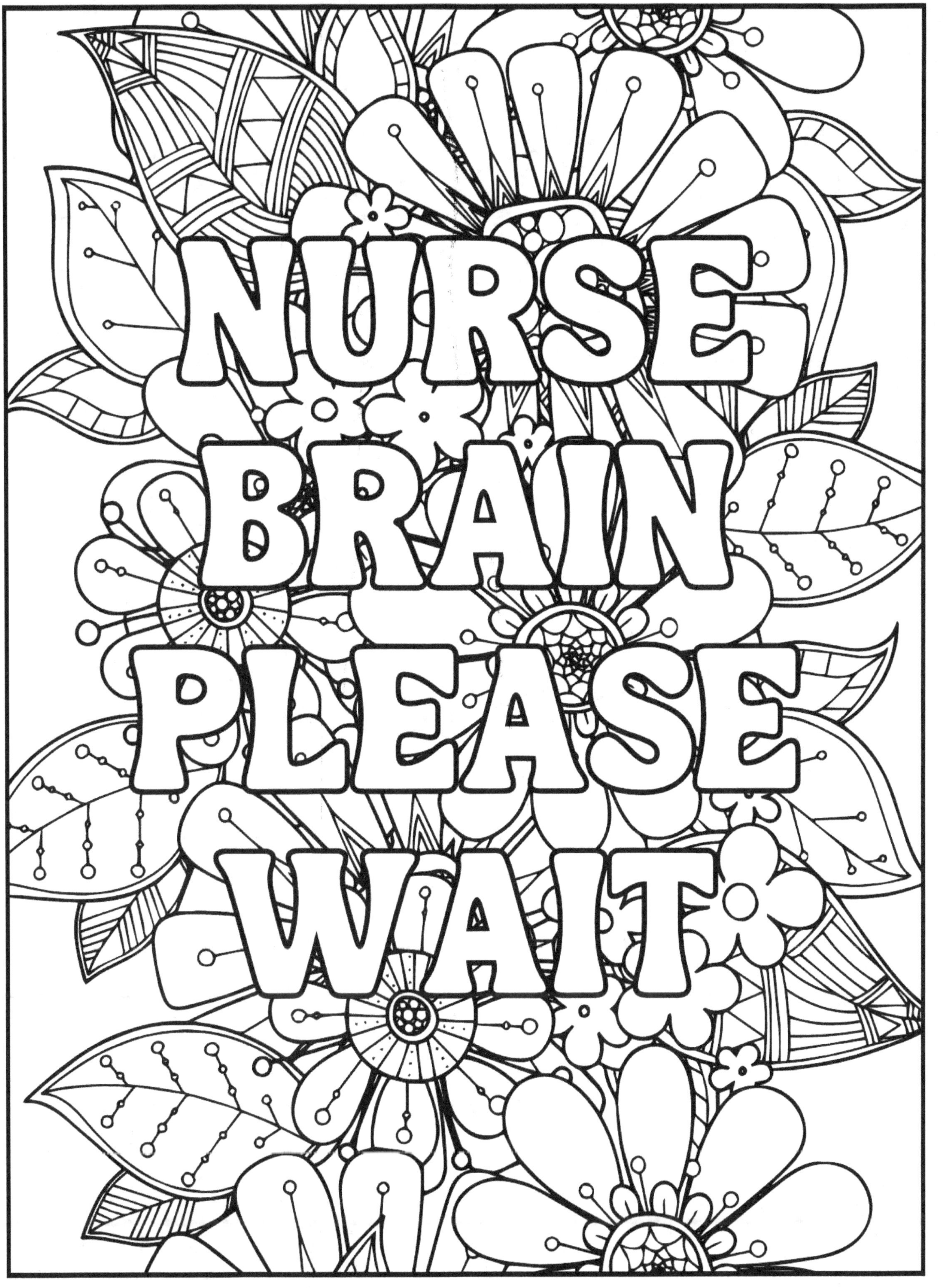
NURSE
BRAIN
PLEASE
WAIT

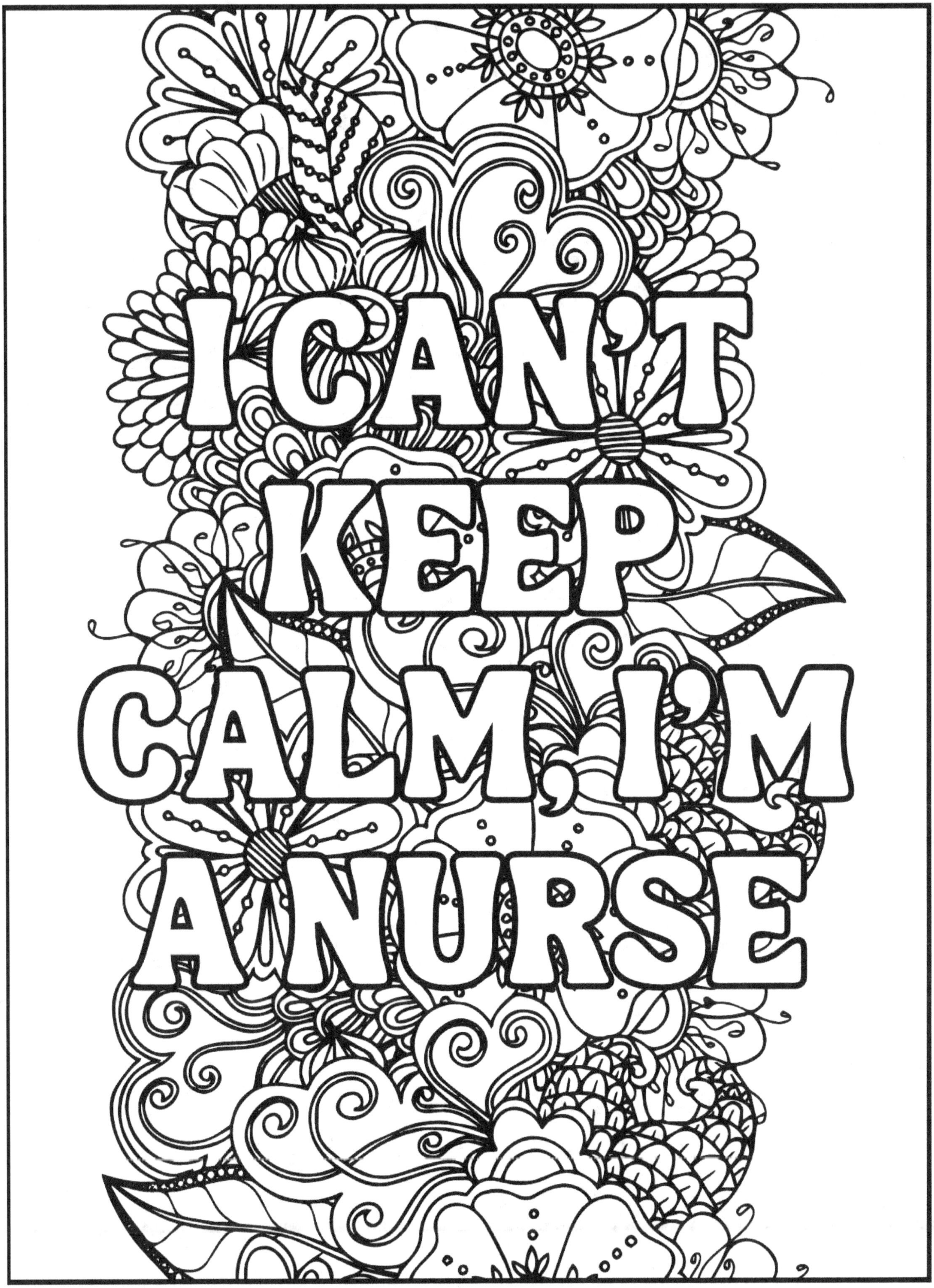
I CAN'T
KEEP
CALM, I'M
A NURSE

www.ingramcontent.com/pod-product-compliance
Lightning Source LLC
Chambersburg PA
CBHW080551240526
45466CB00030B/2857
9798394042034